EXODUS

ROAD TO
FREEDOM

by

Rev. Albert Joseph Mary Shamon

Published by
The Riehle Foundation
P.O. Box 7
Milford, OH 45150-0007 USA
513-576-0032

Nihil obstat: Reverend Robert J. Buschmiller
                  June 29, 1998

Imprimatur: Most Reverend Carl K. Moeddel
                  Vicar General and Auxiliary Bishop
                  Cincinnati, Ohio
                  July 1, 1998

The *Nihil obstat* and the *Imprimatur* are a declaration that a book or pamphlet is considered to be free from doctrinal or moral error. It is not implied that those who have granted the *Nihil obstat* and *Imprimatur* agree with the contents, opinions or statements expressed.

Published by The Riehle Foundation

For additional copies, write:
The Riehle Foundation
P.O. Box 7
Milford, OH 45150-0007 USA

Library of Congress Catalog Card No.: 98-066941

ISBN: 1-877678-50-3

All biblical references were taken from the ST. JOSEPH BIBLE.

Front cover illustration: *The Moses* by Michelangelo in the Basilica of *St. Peter in Chains,* Rome

Cover designed by: **Christian Wilhelmy**

CONTENTS

PREFACE

Genesis is the book of origins. It treats of election: the choosing of God's people.

The Book of Exodus is the book of redemption. It treats of the liberation of God's people.

Exodus, Chapters 1 to 6, pictures Israel in slavery, in need of liberation. Chapters 7 to 11 manifest the power of the Liberator. Chapters 12 to 18 show liberation coming through the blood of the lamb. Chapters 19 to 24 reveal why God liberated His people. But at Sinai they failed Him by worshipping a golden calf, so Chapters 25 to 40 deal with God's mercy toward His people.

Like God's people in Egypt, original sin enslaved us. So God sent, not Moses, but His Son—the Lamb of God—to liberate us. His blood on the doorpost of the cross redeems us. Through the Red Sea of baptism, He frees us from sin. Through the desert of life, He feeds us with manna, bread from heaven, Holy Communion. But, like His people, we often rebel against Him. As He rescued them again and again (Ps 106:43), so He offers us forgiveness again and again through the Sacrament of Reconciliation.

I wish to express my sincere thanks to David and Darlene Duprey for helping with the illustrations in this book.

Good Friday
April 10, 1998

Chapter 1

An Enslaved People

Genesis is the preface to Exodus. Genesis explains why the Hebrews were in Egypt (the Joseph Story— Genesis 37-47), and why God sent Moses to free them from Egyptian slavery (the Covenant with Abraham—Genesis 15).

But more important Genesis shows that man needed a redeemer, a liberator. Chapters three to eleven of Genesis show that after his first sin man was like a person caught in quicksand, he needed outside help. The Book of Exodus shows that this outside help came from God Himself, that this liberator, redeemer, was none other than the God of Abraham, the God of Isaac and the God of Jacob—Yahweh Himself!

Exodus is the second book of the Bible. The word "exodus" comes from two Greek words (ex meaning "out of" and odos meaning "road"). Exodus tells of the Israelites' departure, their going out of Egypt and the road they took.

The Book has four divisions: (1) the Israelites in Egypt (Chapters 1 to 12:36); (2) the exodus from Egypt and the journey to Sinai (Chapters 12:37 to 18:27); (3) the Covenant on Mt. Sinai (Chapters 19:1 to 24:18); and (4) the Covenant broken, renewed, and the provisions made for God's dwelling and its furnishings (Chapters 25:1 to 40:38).

The Book of Exodus is a national epic. It is the story of the birth of a nation. Thus the author does not worry about precision regarding details; rather he paints with large strokes the better to establish his heroes. One can see that the details do not have to be taken literally. We have the essentials. What counts most is the religious meaning of the

1

events.

Exodus is the key book of the Old Testament. It is significant that God's religion did not originate in the mind of some philosopher or thinker, like Buddhism or Mohammedanism. God's religion began with historical events: the Old Testament with the exodus from Egypt around the time of Ramses II, and the New Testament with the birth of Jesus during the reign of Augustus Caesar. Exodus narrates the saving actions of God, namely, His grace, covenant and mercy. These same actions are central to the New Testament. Lastly, Israel is born as a nation on Sinai; the new Israel, the Church, is born in the Upper Room on Pentecost Sunday.

The Book of Exodus reveals much about God. Its first great revelation is Monotheism: "I am the Lord—I, alone, there is no other" (20:3). Second, God is a Person: He uses the personal pronoun "I"—"I am!" (3:14). Third, God is perfectly free in His choices: He chooses Israel through no merits of her own—"I grant mercy to whom I will" (33:19). Fourth, He is good: He does not want people enslaved by other people (3:8).

Moreover, He is faithful: He keeps His promises made to Abraham. He is powerful: invincible Egypt is crushed before Him. He is Provident: He provides for His people in the desert. He seeks obedience (19:5); but He is merciful, for when His people disobey and break the Covenant He forgives them and renews the Covenant (34:10). He is concerned about other peoples, for He chose Israel to be a blessing or a curse and a light to the nations (Gn 12:3; Lk 2:32).

The Historical Context of Exodus. Abraham came to the land of Canaan around 1800 B.C. Jacob went from Canaan to Egypt around 1700 B.C. The Hebrews settled in the land of Goshen, in the Delta area of the Nile, for four centuries. Scripture tells us nothing of these 400 years: it jumps from the death of Joseph at the end of Genesis to the events leading to the Exodus.

During the 400-year interlude, the Hyksos invaded Egypt. They had superior armament and probably introduced the chariot into Egypt. With their superior power, they were able to conquer Egypt in 1675 B.C. Joseph came to Egypt around 1650 B.C. The Hyksos were a mixed people, with a generous proportion of Semitic blood. Thus Semites were accorded preferential treatment. In such an Egypt, it is easy to see how Joseph could have risen to power.

After Joseph and all his brothers had died and the Israelites had become numerous and strong in the land, there came a Pharaoh who knew not Joseph. This Pharaoh was Ahmose I (1570-1564 B.C.), called the George Washington of Egypt. About 1567 B.C. he overthrew the Hyksos and regained Egypt for the Egyptians. Under Thuthmose III (1479-1447 B.C.), called the Napoleon of Egypt, the Semitic element lost their privileged status and even became suspect. The Hebrews were not driven out of Egypt because the Pharaohs had great building programs in mind and the Hebrews offered plentiful and cheap labor. This situation lasted for a few hundred years.

Around the time of Ramses II (1292-1225 B.C.) the capital of Egypt was shifted from Thebes to the Delta. There, Ramses came into direct contact with the Hebrews and enslaved them. Conditions worsened when the Pharaoh commanded that all the male children of the Hebrews be killed. This only lit the desire for freedom in the hearts of the Hebrews.

The Exodus occurred about 1240 B.C. Mernephtah (1225-1215 B.C.), the thirteenth son of Ramses, probably was co-regent with his father at the time of the exodus. (See, Riciotti, Giuseppe. *The History of Israel,* Vol. 1, pp. 24, 191.)

Perseverance in Prayer. The story of Israel's road to freedom illustrates the need for perseverance in prayer. Under Ramses, the Hebrews cried out because of their slavery and their cry went up to God. God heard their cry at once by moving a woman to spare her baby boy, Moses (2:3). Yet at the time the enslaved Israelites did not know that God was already answering their prayers.

Next, God had to prepare Moses to lead His people out of slavery. That preparation would take eighty years. Ironically, God trained Moses as an Egyptian prince in the court of the persecutor of His people. For forty years, Moses was trained in Egyptian politics and diplomacy, in its military skills and its law.

Then for another forty years, as a fugitive in Midian, east of the Gulf of Aqaba, and as the son-in-law of a sheikh of Araby, he learned the art of living in the desert and the science of tribal administration. (Cp. Heb 11:23-27.)

Finally, God had to prepare His people to accept His answer to their prayers. They wanted freedom from slavery; but God wanted much more for them. He wanted them to be permanently free by taking them out of Egypt and making them a nation in a land flowing with milk and honey.

To wean them from their love for Egypt would take eighty years of cruel slavery. Even after this, their attachment to Egypt remained so great that in their desert wanderings they often yearned for the fleshpots of Egypt.

Thus we ought always to persevere in prayer. For often God has to prepare the answer (in this case Moses); and then He has to prepare the pray-ers (the enslaved Israelites) to accept His answer. Delays in prayer must never be interpreted as denials!

Chapter 2

The Call of Moses

The Call of Moses. The call of Moses followed the pattern of prophetic vocations. There was an overpowering vision and a commission.

While tending the flock of his father-in-law Jethro, Moses came to Mt. Horeb. There he saw fire flaming out of a bush; the bush, though on fire, was not consumed. Moses was curious; he decided to investigate and see why the bush was not being burned.

As Moses drew near to the bush, God called out to him from the bush. In the Old Testament fire is the symbol of divinity. First, God told Moses who He was—"I am the God of your father, the God of Abraham, the God of Isaac, and the God of Jacob" (3:6). Then He told him why He had come: "I have heard the cry of my people and I have come to rescue them from the hands of the Egyptians" (3:7-8). Finally, He gave Moses the commission: "I will send you to Pharaoh to lead my people, the Israelites, out of Egypt" (3:10).

As always in His dealings with men, God revealed only the first part of His plan to Moses, namely, his role as liberator. Had He shown Moses all that He had in mind for him to do, Moses would have given in to discouragement. Every vocation is unfolded little by little, step by step. A good rule is to take things a day at a time. "Let each day be content with its own ills" and its own graces. So God asked Moses to take just a first step. Later, at Sinai, God would call Moses to be a ruler and a lawgiver.

As it was, Moses was reluctant to take even the first step. He posed one objection after another as to why he should not do what God was asking him to do.

The Objections of Moses. His first objection stemmed from his preoccupation with himself. Moses declared he was unqualified for the mission. "Who am I that I should go to Pharaoh and lead the Israelites out of Egypt?" Moses was not being modest; his humility went deep. He regarded himself as totally unworthy (Num 12:3). God quashed that objection by promising His own assistance: "I will be with you" (3:12).

Unconvinced, Moses said to God, "When I go to the Israelites and say to them, 'The God of your fathers has sent me to you,' if they ask me, 'What is his name?' what am I to tell them?" "This is what you shall reply to the Israelites, I AM (YHWH) sent me to you" (3:13-14).

To the Hebrews the word YHWH sounded like the third person singular of the Hebrew verb "to be," namely, "He is." Since this verb can be used actively or passively, the name YHWH can have four meanings, none of which excludes the other.

It could mean: "I am the One who causes things to happen." This would assure Moses.

It could mean: "I am the One who is not changeable; the One who is the same always and present always among my people." Again, a reason for confidence.

It could mean: "I am who I am." This could be a refusal to answer the question. "I am whatever you make me or think me to be; I am everything and more than you can conceive of."

Or it could mean simply the two words: "I AM."

The Hebrew name for God was a combination of four consonants YHWH (called the tetragrammaton). From a strained interpretation of Lev 24:16, Hebrews felt that the name of God could be pronounced only once a year by the high priest before the Holy of Holies on the feast of the Day of Atonement. At all other times the Hebrews susbstituted the word ADONAI, which means Lord.

Now a strange thing happened. About the sixth century A.D. when Hebrew ceased to be a spoken language, a guild of Jewish Scribes known as Masoretes (Traditionalists) invented a system of "points"—dots that stood for vowels. As long as Hebrew was a spoken language, consonants alone sufficed; but when it ceased to be spoken, then there was fear that a word would be lost or be mistaken for a wrong word. For instance, take the three consonants BLL—without written vowels they could stand for one of five words: BALL, BELL, BILL, BOLL, BULL. So the Masoretes edited the Bible with vowel signs, the Masoretic text. (Cp. McKenzie, John L. *Dictionary of the Bible,* pp. 880-881.)

However, in the thirteenth century some Christian scholar(s) made a big mistake when it came to putting vowels into the four consonants for the name God. We know from Greek texts back in the second century that the vowels for the word God were "a" and "e"—Yahweh. But some thirteenth century Scripture scholars didn't know that so they took the vowels from the word ADONAI and added them to the four consonants for God.

The first vowel for ADONAI sounds like a mute "e," the second like an "o," and the third like an "a"; the "Y" of the tetragrammaton was pronounced as "J." As a result we got the hybrid word for God, the mistaken word, JEHOVAH, instead of the correct name YAHWEH! (Anderson, Richard. *Understanding the Old Testament,* pp.33-34; Grollenberg, Luke H. *Interpreting the Bible,* pp. 54-55; Riciotti, Giuseppe. Idem, Vol. 1, pp. 177-179.)

The root of YHWH is the verb "to be." Thus God gave Moses His name as "I AM." Etienne Gilson called this the greatest definition of God in all history. Just consider for a moment all those two words connote, all they tell us about God.

The "I" tells us that God is a PERSON! Not a stick,

a stone, or a senseless thing as are the gods of heathendom. For the pagan gods are the handiwork of men: having eyes that do not see; ears that do not hear; feet that cannot walk (Ps 115).

The "AM" tells us that God exists. There IS a God. Also, the "AM" is the present tense of the verb "to be" as if to tell us that God has no past, no future, just a present. Thus He coexists with all times and persons. He is the God of Abraham, the God of Isaac, the God of Jacob, a span of a couple hundred years. As the center of a circle is abreast with every point on the circumference, so God is abreast with all times, but He Himself is timeless. In other words, "AM" tells us God is ETERNAL!

Furthermore, "AM" is the verb "to be"; it tells us God is BEING par excellence. Imperfection is a lack of being. A hole in a fence is a lack of fence. Blindness is a lack of sight. Deafness is a lack of hearing. But because God is BEING, He has no lack; therefore, no imperfection. In other words, He is ALL-PERFECT!

One final point on this matter. Suppose you asked me, "Who are you?" I would answer, "I'm a priest." That is true, but that limits me. Supppose I asked you, "Who are you?" You would answer either "I'm a wife"; or "I'm a husband"; or "I'm a doctor"; or "a lawyer"; or "a scientist"; or "a teacher"—no matter, any answer limits each of us. Moses asked God, "Who are you?" God answered, "I AM" period! No qualification, no limit. So, an INFINITE BEING!

When St. John wanted to bring out Jesus' divinity in his gospel, he used the seven great "I am's." "I am the bread of life"; "I am the light of the world"; "I am the Good Shepherd"; etc. (cp. Jn 8:24, 28; 13:19). When the Jews asked Jesus how he could have seen Abraham since he wasn't even fifty years old, Jesus replied, "Before Abraham came to be, I AM." And the Jews picked up stones to throw at Him, for He had identified Himself with God (Jn 8:57; 10:31).

Moses still tried to extricate himself. He objected that nobody would believe him. "Suppose they will not believe me, nor listen to my plea?"

In answer God gave Moses two signs. First, He changed Moses' staff into a serpent. The serpent was the symbol of Egypt (the Pharaoh wore a serpent in his headdress). God implied that the serpent, Egypt, would become in his hand like his staff, a thing easy to handle (cp. Is 10:5).

The second sign was leprosy, the most dreaded disease in the East. God afflicted Moses' hand with leprosy and then cured him. Thus Yahweh showed Moses that Yahweh has absolute power. He is a God who can strike and who can cure.

So Moses made one last try. "Lord," he said, "I have never been eloquent....I am slow of speech and tongue" (4:10). God answered, "I will assist you and teach you what you are to say." But Moses insisted, "Send soneone else." Graciously, God acceded in part, "Aaron your brother is eloquent, he will be your mouthpiece."

To allay any further fears, God assured Moses that "all the men who sought your life are dead" (4:19).

How often God chooses the weak to do His great deeds. Moses was fearful, hesitant, unwilling, and unbelieving, yet God used him! If God were to wait until He found a person who was worthy or fit to be used by Him, He would have to wait forever. The great "I am" can do anything He wishes and with anyone He chooses. God always fits the back to the task. What is needed is trust. Trust enables us to put God between us and our difficulties instead of putting difficulties between God and us.

Chapter 3

God Takes on Pharaoh and His Gods
(Exodus 7-11)

After the incident of the burning bush Moses returned to Egypt with his wife Zipporah, their children, and the staff of God. The Lord said to him, "On your return to Egypt, see that you perform before Pharaoh all the wonders I have put in your power" (4:21). At Sinai Aaron joined Moses and together they assembled the elders of the Israelites and told them all that the Lord had said to Moses. After that Moses and Aaron went to Pharaoh and confronted him and his magicians.

The malice of Pharaoh and his evil were manifested in his refusal to grant Moses' first request. All Moses asked of Pharaoh was that he let the Israelites go not out of Egypt, but just into the wilderness, for three days to offer sacrifice to the Lord. The request was perfectly reasonable. Even heathens believed that a people should be permitted to worship their god after their accepted manner. Pharaoh not only scorned their request but increased their labors.

So often things get worse for those seeking to follow God before they get better. Not only did Pharaoh turn on the people, but the people turned against Moses. God permits all this to demonstrate to the evildoers how long-suffering He is and to ready the afflicted to appreciate more deeply His deliverance when it should come.

After this initial conflict, God took on the Pharaoh and his gods in full force. The gauntlet was flung. God picked it up and sent disasters upon the land and the Egyptians in such great numbers that in the end Pharaoh and the Egyptians were glad to see the Israelites leave their land.

The disasters God wreaked in Egypt have been systematized into a schema of ten plagues:

1. water to blood	6. boils
2. frogs	7. hail
3. gnats	8. locusts
4. flies	9. darkness
5. cattle plague	10. death of first-born

The first nine of these plagues were natural phenomena occurring in the Nile valley in the spring months. The Nile flooding is caused by Abyssinian rains. The flooding brings microcosma (flagellates) and red soil from Abyssinia and these redden the Nile waters, killing all the fish and raising a horrible stench.

The Nile flooding also caused the second plague of frogs infected with anthrax. The frog was an object of worship among the Egyptians so God caused them to plague the Egyptians by invading not only their land but even their homes. Their ugly shape, their croaking noise, and their disagreeable smell made them obnoxious.

The swamplands and the marshes caused by the flooding bred mosquitoes and flies that spread virus or bacteria to animals and men causing pestilence among the animals and boils on men. February brings hail and thunderstorms which destroy flax and barley but leave wheat and spelt untouched. The wheat and the spelt the locusts destroyed. Then the March winds that blow cause the silt deposited by the flood to rise in clouds of fine dust that caused a darkness so thick you could feel it. The final and most terrible plague was the death of the first-born of the Egyptians and even of the animals.

All these plagues, with the exception of the tenth, were natural occurrences well-known to the Egyptians. Their miraculous character lay in the circumstances which accompanied them: for instance, they were produced instantaneously when Moses wished them; they occurred at unusual times; they were more severe than usual; and the Hebrews themselves were spared.

God produced these prodigies to manifest His mighty power to all; to punish Pharaoh and the Egyptians for their harsh treatment of the Hebrews; and to teach His own people that He not only exists but that He is faithful to His promises and is moved by human suffering. It was Israel's need, not her worth, that drew God to act on her behalf, for He is "a merciful and gracious God...rich in kindness and fidelity" (34:6). So His characteristic action in Exodus is deliverance.

Finally, the plagues also teach us that God is not indifferent to sin. For a long time He puts up with evil, but in the end His wrath descends upon the evildoers. "At midnight the Lord slew every first-born in the land of Egypt,...and there was loud wailing througout Egypt, for there was not a house without its dead" (12:29-30). And shortly after, "Pharaoh's chariots and army he hurled into the sea" (15:4). Thus the Psalmist urges us to heed the words of God: "Today if you hear the voice of the Lord, harden not your hearts..." (Ps 95:7-8). For "it is a fearful thing to fall into the hands of the living God" (Heb 10:31).

Chapter 4

The Tenth Plague

God showed His mercy in restricting nine of the ten plagues to the land and to the discomfort of the people. But when these disasters only hardened the heart of Pharaoh, God turned on the people themselves in the tenth plague. The Lord told Moses, "One more plague will I bring upon Pharaoh and upon Egypt....At midnight I will go forth through Egypt. Every first-born in this land shall die, from the first-born of Pharaoh to the first-born of the slave-girl, as well as all the first-born of the animals" (11:1-5).

The first-born of the Israelites were spared by means of a substitute. The blood of an innocent victim, a lamb without blemish, saved the Israelites. Moses told the elders of Israel to procure lambs for their families and slaughter them. Then they were to dip a bunch of hyssop in their blood and sprinkle it on the lintel and the two doorposts. Seeing the blood on the lintel and doorposts the angel of death would pass over those homes and spare their first-born.

The people did as the Lord had commanded them through Moses and Aaron. At midnight the Lord slew every first-born of the land of Egypt, but passed over the homes of the Israelites sprinkled with the blood of lambs.

This ritual in connection with the Passover in Egypt was very striking. First, there had to be a killing—the shedding of blood; and second, there had to be a sprinkling of the blood on the doorposts and lintels of the homes where the Israelites were dwelling that night. "Without the shedding of the blood, there is no forgiveness" (Heb 9:22); without the sprinkling of the blood, there is no salvation. The death and sprinkling of blood are very different. Death satisfied the justice of God: the death of the first-born for the guilty Egyptians; and the death of a substitute, a lamb, for the innocent Israelites. The sprinkling of blood saved the Israelites. Both were needed.

This double action typified clearly the redemptive act of Jesus. He died; His death satisfied the justice of God and saved the world (propitiation). But His death was not enough. If it were to redeem the sinner, it needed to be appropriated by the sinner through baptism and Eucharist (appropriation). Like a great physician, Christ's death was a cure-all medicine; but to benefit the sick person, it had to be taken. (Cp. Pink, Arthur. *Gleanings in Exodus,* p. 84.)

For those in Egypt who did not sprinkle the blood of the lamb on their doorposts and lintels, there was only death. Loud was the wailing throughout Egypt. That very night Pharaoh summoned Moses and Aaron and bade them lead their people out of Egypt. Before leaving, Moses commanded the Israelites to ask the Egyptians for articles of silver and gold and for clothing. The Egyptians let them have whatever they asked for. "Thus did they despoil the Egyptians" (12:36).

Again here we see the justice of God at work. What the Israelites took from the Egyptians was owed them. It was a just recompense for the years of slave labor in the brick-kilns of Egypt. They were entitled to what they took. Remember in the Civil War, the North wondered why it dragged out so many years when the manpower, wealth, and materiel were all on the side of the North. Lincoln in his Second Inaugural Address gave the answer: "God wills it to continue until all the wealth piled by the bondman's two hundred and fifty years of unrequited toil shall be sunk, and until every drop of blood drawn with the lash shall be paid by another drawn with the sword,..." For God is a just judge. So Egypt was made to pay for decades of unrequited toil.

Three feasts emerged from this emancipation of Israel from Egypt: the feast of the Passover, the feast of Azymes, and the feast of the Presentation of the first-born of men and of animals to the Lord. The origin of the Passover feast is obscure. It was probably an ancient nomad festival related to the spring departure of nomads for pastures. This was celebrated by sacrificing the first-born of the flocks to God. The purpose of the feast was to ward off demonic powers by a blood-rite with the lamb. Perhaps it was to celebrate some such rite that the Hebrews kept asking Pharaoh to let them go into the desert to offer sacrifices.

At the time of the exodus, this festival was attached to the historical event of the exodus and interpreted in the light of this event.

The regulations governing the Passover sacrifice (Exodus 12) come from after the Babylonian Exile (539 B.C.).

The Passover was celebrated in the first month of the new year, the 14th day of Abib, later called Nisan (the Spring Equinox). It is primarily a family feast (hence the regulations in 12:43-49). The head of the family led the rite: an unblemished lamb was slaughtered, its blood smeared on the tent flap or doorpost, its flesh roasted (the quickest way of cooking). Since the lamb was a consecrated victim, its bones were not broken, and leftovers were burned the next morning. The bitter herbs came to symbolize the bitterness of the oppression in Egypt, and the girt loins and sandalled feet (instead of the usual bare feet), and the staff for walking, recalled the haste of the last meal in Egypt before departure.

Once the Hebrews reached the Promised Land another feast was added to the feast of the Passover: the feast of Mazzoth or Azymes (Unleavened Bread). The Canaanites, an agricultural people, celebrated a feast of

Azymes in the springtime. When the Hebrews settled in the Promised Land, they took this feast and joined it to their Passover feast and interpreted it in the light of the exodus event.

The exodus event was a hasty departure from Egypt. Leaven symbolized delay: it takes time for leaven to cause the dough to rise. Unleavened bread, on the contrary, symbolized haste—the haste with which the Hebrews left Egypt.

Later, leaven came to symbolize sourness, decay, corruption, and decomposition—for it broke down the dough. As such, it was to be left behind in Egypt and a new start made. Since the feast fell at the time of the barley harvest, it involved starting a new year without any traces of the sourness or decay of the previous year's produce. The corrupt state of leavened food explains why only unleavend bread could be offered to YHWH in sacrifice.

Unleaven symbolized innocence and wholesomeness. Thus St. Paul wrote: "Our paschal lamb, Christ, has been sacrificed. Therefore let us celebrate the feast, not with the old yeast, the leaven of malice and wickedness, but with the unleavened bread of sincerity and truth" (1 Cor 5:7-8).

In light of the fact that God had spared the first-born of the Hebrews at the time of the exodus, the redemption of the first-born was mentioned here (Chapter 11). The Lord spoke to Moses and said, "Consecrate to me every first-born that opens the womb among the Israelites, both of man and beast for it belongs to me" (13:2).

The sin of the angels was pride; the sin of man is amnesia. So God demanded that the first-born be consecrated to Him that His people might not forget the wonders He had wrought for them in Egypt. Thus Mary and Joseph presented the first-born Jesus to the Lord in the temple forty days after His birth (Lk 2:22-35).

Chapter 5

The Road to Freedom

The exodus, or departure from Egypt, took place about 1240 B.C. when powerful Ramses II (1292-1225 B.C.) occupied the throne of Egypt. Scripture says, "The Israelites set out from Ramses for Succoth, about six hundred thousand men on foot, not counting the children" (Ex 12:37).

The figure six hundred thousand is obviously an exaggeration, for it does not square with the information in Exodus 1:15-20 that two midwives served the whole Hebrew colony. Moreover, the Delta area could not have accommodated that many Hebrews. Then too how could six hundred thousand have crossed the Sea of Reeds in a single night? Furthermore, when the Hebrews fought the Amalekites, the battle was indecisive for a while (17:8). And the Amalekites army did not number more than five to seven thousand. Israel's army therefore must have been about six thousand strong (Keller, Werner. *The Bible As History*, pp. 141-42). Very likely the number leaving Egypt was about twenty-five thousand, that is, six thousand men plus the women and the children. (Cp. Riciotti, *Idem,* pp. 192-193.)

The route of the fleeing Israelites cannot be determined with any certainty. The shortest route would have been along the Mediterranean seacoast, "by way of the Philistines' land" (13:17). This was the main highway from Egypt to Asia via Palestine for caravans and military expeditions and ran parallel with the Mediterranean coast. But this route was closely guarded by an army of soldiers and officials in strong frontier posts who kept a sharp eye on all traffic in both directions. "Should the people see that they would have to fight, they might change their minds and return to Egypt" (13:17). So the Israelites headed southward by way of the desert road, the longer, but the safer route. They journeyed from Rameses to Succoth (12:37) to Etham (13:20) to Pihahiroth between Migdol and the Reed Sea (14:2). (Grollenberg, Luke. *Atlas of the Bible,* p. 48.)

Pharaoh believed that the Hebrews were lost and were wandering aimlessly. So he sent his army out to recover his work force. The situation of the Hebrews was desperate: they were literally caught between the devil and the deep blue (Reed) sea. And they reacted typically: they complained. The theme of Israel's "murmuring" begins here (14:11). Moses responded: "Fear not! Stand your ground, and you will see the victory the Lord will win for you today....The Lord himself will fight for you; you have only to keep still" (14:13-14).

"Then Moses stretched out his hand over the sea, and the Lord swept the sea with a strong east wind throughout the night and so turned it into dry land. When the water was thus divided, the Israelites marched into the midst of the sea on dry land, with the water like a wall to their right and to their left" (14:21-22).

The Egyptian forces followed in pursuit. Moses stretched out his hand over the sea and the waters flowed back annihilating Pharaoh's entire army.

The sea that was crossed was probably the Sea of Reeds. The miracle there had both natural and supernatural elements.

The natural elements were the winds and the tides. The passage was probably made south of the Bitter Lakes, which was joined to the Red Sea by a strand of water bordered by marshlands, called the Sea of Reeds subject to tides. Ebb tide and a strong easterly wind made a passage possible. The morning fog clouded the vision of the Egyptians, the swampy land clogged their chariot wheels, and the violent return of the tide engulfed them.

The supernatural elements were the column of cloud and fire, guiding the Israelites, the foreknowledge by Moses of the waters parting and returning, this all happening at the very moment needed to deliver Israel from her critical situation, the ebb tide staying out long enough to permit all the Hebrews to cross, and its flowing back at the precise moment needed to engulf the Egyptians.

The account of the event is in epic style, embellished by later retelling. No one doubts the essential facts of the Exodus story: the oppression, the leadership of Moses, and the deliverance by Yahweh's power. However, not all the details are to be taken literally, such as "water standing like a wall." Details are secondary to the meaning of the story. The point the authors wished to make clear is that God's intervention, not the prowess of the Israelites, secured the victory.

Israel's response to this saving action of God was song and dance: the Song of Moses and the dance and Song of Miriam (15:1-21). Their thanksgiving hymns did more than exult over fallen enemies. They expressed the discoveries Israel had made about her God: His power, uniqueness, love, kingship; His special relationship to Israel; and a faith now that believed that He who could humble mighty Egypt would be more than a match for the petty princedoms of Canaan.

Moses' victory chant is sung at the Easter vigil and also resounds in Heaven together with the canticle of the Lamb (Rv 15:3).

In the first fifteen chapters of Exodus we are very likely dealing with an account developed as reading for the Passover festival to commemorate the deliverance from Egypt. The historical event has been embellished, so to speak, by details which emphasize the saving power of Yahweh. So the literary form of these chapters is not so much history in our sense of the word, but a cult epic, literature influenced by liturgy.

The exodus foreshadowed the much greater work of the exodus of Jesus. In our Lord's transfiguration on Mt. Tabor Moses and Elijah appeared with Jesus and they "spoke of His exodus that he was going to accomplish in Jerusalem" (Lk 9:31). In the first exodus Moses led the Hebrews out of slavery; the blood of the lamb sprinkled on the lintel and doorposts of their homes saved the lives of their first-born children, and they were led to a land of milk and honey. But Jesus' exodus was going to be His death, resurrection, and ascension. He was the Lamb of God whose blood sprinkled on the doorpost of the cross would free, not just the Hebrews, but all mankind from the slavery of Satan and sin. It would give all mankind the freedom of the sons of God and ultimately lead them to the promised land of eternal life in Heaven.

Chapter 6

To Sinai

After crossing the Reed Sea, a hard journey awaited the Israelites. They would have to live a nomadic life in barren scrubland for forty years. With donkeys, goats, and sheep, they could cover only about twelve miles a day, going from one water hole to the next. The Book of Numbers in Chapter 33 gives a broad outline of their route.

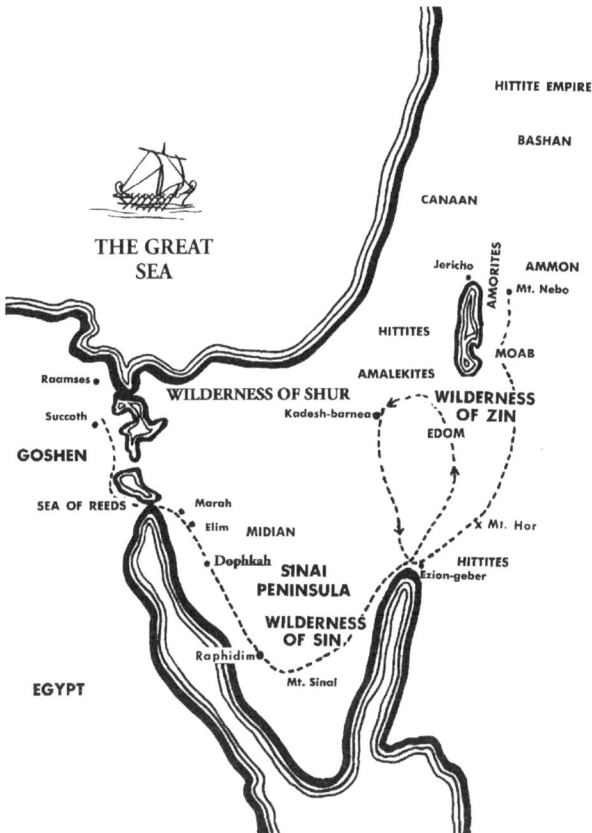

Exodus From Egypt Around 1240 B.C.

Once they had crossed the Reed Sea, they set out southward for the Wilderness of Sinai, for Moses had been commissioned to bring the people to worship God on Mt. Sinai (3:12). They followed a well-worn track leading to Sinai. The track had been made by labor gangs and slave gangs working the mines in the Sinai Mountains digging for copper and turquoise for Ramses II.

In the first stage of their southward journey, they traveled three days for forty-five miles through the desert of Shur without finding water. When they arrived at Marah, the water there was salty and sulphurous. The Bible says the waters were "bitter" and undrinkable. The people grumbled against Moses. He went to the Lord who told him to throw a branch of a tree into the water. The branch was probably from a barberry tree, now extinct in that area, which had a purifying and sweetening power (15:22-25).

"Then they came to Elim, where there were twelve springs of water and seventy palm trees, and they camped there near the water" (15:27).

After Elim, they entered the Wilderness of Sin that reached to the shore of the Reed Sea. Here again the Israelites grumbled against Moses. They had not come a great distance, but they were unused to privations after their well-fed and well-ordered life in Egypt. They complained, "Would that we had died in the land of Egypt, as we sat by our fleshpots and ate our fill of bread!" (16:3).

The Lord responded by two great miracles: His sending quail for meat and manna for bread (16:4-15).

In springtime it was not unusual to find quail on the shore of the Reed Sea. They would migrate from Africa to Europe to avoid the unbearable heat and dryness of Africa in summer. After their long flight across the Sea, they would fall exhausted on the flat seashore edging the Wilderness of Sin, to gather fresh strength for the next stage of their journey. Even today in the springtime, Bedouins in this area catch exhausted quails by hand.

As for the manna, tamarisk trees and bushes when pierced by a certain type of shell-backed insect which is found in Sinai produce a secretion much like manna. But the entire Sinai peninsula would hardly produce six hundred pounds of this "manna" a year. Moreover such "manna" was neither tasty nor nutritious.

No matter how people may try to explain the quails on the seashore or the manna, the Hebrews knew for certain that all was done by the hand of God, and that God was active at every point in their escape from Egypt. They knew for certain that He was a liberating God who led, upheld, and provided for the needs of His people. They knew that ultimately their survival depended on God, and that without Him Israel was nothing and could do nothing.

The miracle of the manna teaches that God provides and that it is folly to worry about tomorrow. On the sixth day God gave the Israelites a double portion of manna so that the seventh day might be a day consecrated to the Sabbath rest.

From the Wilderness of Sin the Israelites journeyed on and came to Dophkah (Nm 33:12), a place where the minerals taken from the mines in this area during the reign of Ramses II were smelted. Here archaeologists found some stone tablets with writing on them different from hieroglyphics and cuneiform writing. The tablets proved that around 1500 B.C. a system of linear writing existed in Canaan from which our own alphabet ultimately developed. Also it proved that the Israelites were literate at the time of the exodus. (See, Keller,Werner. *The Bible As History,* pp. 125-140.)

It is significant that at this spot God told Moses to write an account of the exodus events. "Write this down in a document as something to be remembered, and recite it in the ears of Joshua" (17:14). It is worthy of note that in this nomadic group there was being formed a collection of documents—"write this down in a document"; and that what was written was to be supported by oral traditions— "recite it in the ears of Joshua."

From the Desert of Sin the Israelites journeyed to and encamped at Rephidim, extolled by Arabs as the "Pearl of Sinai" (17:1). It has a grove of palm trees and abundant water; but at this time the wadi was dry. As usual, the people quarreled with Moses. Moses, as always, turned to the Lord who told him to strike a rock with his staff. He did and water flowed from the rock for all, men and beasts, to drink. The place was called Massah (temptation) and Meribah (strife), because the Israelites quarreled here and tested the Lord.

Often Midianites would find water by striking a rock. Maybe Moses learned this when he lived among them. Limestone when it is weathered is often covered by a smooth hard crust; when the crust is knocked off, the soft stone underneath is exposed and out of its apertures shoot powerful streams of water.

The Amalekites who controlled the caravan trails between Egypt and Palestine and lived in this area attacked the Israelites to defend their wadi against foreign invaders. Moses sent Joshua against them with a courageous band.

As they engaged in battle, Moses along with Aaron and Hur went up a hill to pray. As was customary Moses lifted up his hands to pray. "Hear…my pleading when I cry to you, lifting up my hands" (Ps 28:2). "As long as Moses kept his hands raised up, Israel had the better of the fight, but when he let his hands rest, Amalek had the better of the fight" (17:11). So Aaron and Hur made Moses sit and supported his hands raised in prayer until the battle was won.

As Moses' hands grew heavy so we often grow weary of praying. The support of the Church and friends are often needed to help us to go on. Our Lord told us "to pray always without becoming weary" (Lk 18:1). Perseverance is the key to effective prayer. Then, too, prayer needs to be backed by action, like Joshua fighting against Amalek. We ought to pray as if all depended on God and we ought to act as if all depended on us.

Many lessons can be found in these interventions of God for Israel along the road.

The manna, which ceased after the entrance to Canaan, shows that nourishment comes from God. The manna is also a type of the Eucharist, our food in the journey of life to the promised land of Heaven.

The wood thrown into the bitter waters at Marah foreshadowed the wood of the cross thrown into the bitter sea of the world to heal the bitterness of sin.

The rock giving water is a type of Christ from whose side flowed blood (Eucharist) and water (baptism).

"All drank the same spiritual drink, for they drank from a spiritual rock that followed them, and the rock was the Christ" (1 Cor 10:4).

Chapter 18 in Exodus is obviously out of place here. Chronologically, Moses' setting up an organization for administering justice would fit in better after the sojourn at Sinai (Dt 1:9-18). Moses appoints God-fearing men and puts them in charge of the people as officers over groups of thousands, of hundreds, of fifties, of tens. They were to render decisions for the people in all ordinary cases. The more difficult and important cases were to be referred to Moses himself. Thus this sharing of his work load would prolong Moses' life and vocation. The liberator now becomes a ruler and soon he will become a lawgiver.

We have here an early example of how helpful the laity can be in doing God's work. Moses' sharing his work with others freed him to do more important work and saved him from being worn out. Sharing his work with others was also a boon to the people who were served, for two heads are often better than one. Furthermore, sharing his work with others helped the workers themselves, for one learns by doing. All in all, distributive justice is far better than monopoly, especially in government.

Sinai and the Monastery of Catherine.
(Beadnell, Wilderness of Sinai.)

Chapter 7

The Birth of a Nation

After the journey from Rephidim the Israelites came to the plains of Sinai (19:2). There they pitched their camp on the plain at the foot of the sacred mountain Jebel Musa (Arabic for "Mount of Moses").

At the beginning of the Christian era many monks and hermits built tiny cells to live here. A little chapel was erected at the foot of the mountain. But the barbaric tribes of nomads gave the monks no rest; many were killed. In 327 when St. Helena, the 80-year-old mother of Constantine the Great, came to Jerusalem and learned of the plight of the monks, she had a monastery built for them. In A.D. 530 the Emperor Justinian fortified the chapel there. Devout pilgrims came from every land and stayed at the monastery that is called today the monastery of St. Catherine.

In 1859 the German scripture scholar Constantine von Tischendorf discovered in the Monastery of St. Catherine at Sinai one of the most precious parchment manuscripts of the Bible, the famous Codex Sinaiticus. It dates from the fourth century of the Christian era and contains the New Testament and parts of the Old Testament.

The Czar of Russia accepted it as a gift and gave the monastery 9,000 rubles for it. It was stored in the library at St. Petersburg. But in 1933 the British Museum bought the Codex Sinaiticus from the Soviets for 100,000 pounds.

In this area where the Monastery of St. Catherine is located the Israelites **spent a whole year. All the events in the last half of the Book of Exodus, all the Book of Leviticus and the first ten chapters of the Book of Numbers occurred here while the Israelites camped on**

the plain. Here God made this people a nation, binding them to one another by a Covenant bond (19:3-6).

The traditions concerning the events at Sinai no doubt were preserved in the liturgy of Israel. The Covenant was renewed often (Jos 24), and at such renewals the events of Israel's history were recalled and relived.

In Chapters 19-24, all the elements of liturgy can be found: the ritual purification of the people, the processions, the trumpet blasts to meet God, the presentation of Yahweh, the reading of the Law, and the ratification of the Covenant. Most likely, the historical events at Sinai, as they were understood, were liturgically re-enacted by the people of Israel.

At Sinai, when Moses went up the mountain, God said, "Tell the Israelites, 'If you hearken to my voice and keep my covenant...you shall be to me a holy nation'" (19:3-6).

What is a covenant? The word "covenant" means "cutting." Covenants were ratified by cutting an animal in two and both parties walking between the split parts as if to say, "If we do not keep our part of the covenant, let us be cut in two like the animal" (Gen 15:10). Then the animal was roasted and both parties banqueted as a token of friendship.

Basically, a covenant is a contract. Contracts can be of two kinds. First, a bilateral contract or a parity covenant, that is, an agreement between equals. Such a covenant with God is impossible since God has no equal.

Second, a unilateral contract or a royal covenant, that is, an agreement between unequals, as between a king and his subjects or a master and his servants. One party stipulates the terms, the other party is free to accept or reject them. God's Covenant on Mt. Sinai was a royal covenant. He stipulated the terms of the Covenant, the Ten Commandments; and He promised that if the people kept these, He would dwell among them as their guide and protector.

A covenant usually introduced a dispensation. A "dispensation" originally meant the rules used to run a house: rules to live by. The Covenant on Mt. Sinai introduced rules that Israel was to live by to be God's people—the Law of Moses!

God's Covenant with His people made on Mt. Sinai had the following characteristics: First, it was God who took the intiative: "The Lord called Moses" (19:3).

Second, God freely chose Israel through no merits of her own. "I will show favors to whom I will" (33:19).

Third, His Covenant was conditional: "If you hearken to my voice" (19:5; 34:11). Yet it was irrevocable. God's fidelity is independent of people. Still, fidelity was the condition for His protection. If Israel failed Him, as they often did, God in His mercy allowed them to renew the Covenant by being repentant (34:6-7).

Fourth, the Covenant was universal; it was not for the benefit of Israel alone, but for all nations. "You shall be to me a kingdom of priests" (19:6); that is, a community of ministers called to serve the Lord and be a light to all nations.

Fifth, the Covenant was voluntary. "Everything the Lord has said we will do" (19:8).

Lastly, the mediator between Yahweh and His people was Moses.

From about 1500 to 1200 B.C., the Hittites were a major power in the Middle East. Their capital city was in Asia Minor, but their influence extended even to Canaan where some of them dwelt.

When some treaties of the Hittite kings were discovered, it was found that the Covenant on Mt. Sinai followed the format of these treaties. The Hittite treaties were royal covenants. These followed a well-defined literary pattern. For instance, they began with a preamble, stating the name and the excellence of the king. (Cp. "I, the Lord, am your God" 20:2.)

Then there followed a historical prologue of all the benevolent actions of the king done in behalf of his vassals (cp. Ex 19:4).

Next, in gratitude for the king's benevolence, there was a listing of obligations which the vassals were asked to assume, chief of which was not to make pacts with any other power. (Cp. "You shall not have other gods besides me" 20:3.)

This treaty was witnessed and deposited for safekeeping in some sacred spot, like a temple. (Cp. The tablets of the Law were kept in the Ark, Ex 40:20; Dt 31:24.)

The document ended with curses on those who broke the treaty and blessings on those who kept it. (Cp. Ex 23:20-33; Dt 11:26ff; 27:14ff.)

In the light of the discovery of the Hittite royal treaties, we can see that Chapters 1 to 19 of Exodus written before the Covenant were meant to show the graciousness, kindness, and might of the Lord in behalf of Israel. This preparation for the giving of the Law had the same purpose as the prologue in Hittite treaties which listed the benevolent acts of their kings. It was expected that Israel would accept the Laws of the Covenant in grateful recognition of the goodness of the Lord toward herself. Obeying the Law was to be an act of gratitude to God who found a people helpless in slavery and brought them out of the house of bondage. In this context, the Law was not the first element in the Old Testament—God's graciousness was!

On Mt. Sinai God set forth the obligations of Israel in two bodies of laws: the Ten Commandmets (Ex 20:1-17; Dt 5:6-21); and the Code of the Covenant (20:22—23:19).

The Code of the Covenant, or the Law of Moses, constitutes all the legislation, judicial and ceremonial, which God gave Israel during its sojourn in the wilderness and which was developed in the time of Judges when Israel was in the Promised Land (20:22-23:19).

The Code deals with real life cases, selects a few criminal cases and prescribes the penalty. Some of these laws have a striking resemblance to ancient codes, like that of Hammurabi (1700 B.C.).

This Code of the Covenant was inserted by the editors of Exodus right after the Ten Commandments (Chapters 21-23) to indicate that these laws too were part of the revelation given to Moses on Mt. Sinai. However, unlike the Ten Commandments, the Code, the Law of Moses, as such, bound no one but the Israelites. It was not valid for all times and in all places (cp. Rom 6:15; 7; Gal 3:19).

The Ten Commandments differ from the Code of the Covenant. The Ten Commandments, the ten short words (decalogue), are the Law of God. They express the mind and will of the Creator and bind all mankind for all times and in all places. They are the basis for individual and social morality.

To show their importance, the Commandments were promulgated by the voice of God amid the most solemn manifestations and tokens of God's presence. They were written directly by the finger of God and were written upon tables of stone to denote their lasting and imperishable nature. Finally, the Ten Commandments were the only laws of Israel that were put into the Ark of the Covenant.

Why are there exactly Ten Commandments and not seven or twelve? One simple reason could be that every man has ten fingers. Thus five of the commandments pertaining to the rights of God could be counted on one hand and five pertaining to the rights of man could be counted on the other hand. When the two hands are folded, they express that the rights of God and the rights of man go hand in hand! (Grollenberg, Luke H. *Interpreting the Bible,* pp. 17-20.)

The Jewish and Protestant listing of the Ten Commandments differs from that of the Catholic listing. Catholics accepted the Ten Commandments as listed in Dt 5:6-21. There the worship of God and the prohibition of idolatry are put together under the First Commandment. Jews, however, preferred the listing of the Commandments in Ex 20:2-17. In this listing the prohibition of idolatry is presented as the Second Commandment. The Jews preferred this listing, because idolatry was a real danger for them, as in the case of the golden calf (Ex 32:7-10).

In the Deuteronomy listing, accepted by Catholics, the coveting of a neighbor's wife and the coveting of his goods are separated to become the Ninth and Tenth Commandments. The Jews, on the contrary, united these two items into one commandment: their tenth, for in the desert wanderings nomads had no houses nor lands that could be coveted.

Protestants followed the Jewish listing, taken from Philo and Josephus, and based on the Exodus version (Ex 20:2-17). The Catholic listing follows St. Augustine, who based his listing of the Commandments on the version in the Book of Deuteronomy (5:6-21), which took into account the settled conditions of Israel in Canaan.

God showed His wisdom by couching the Ten Commandments in negatives; that is, by beginning each law with "Thou shalt not." When a mother speaks to her child, she uses negatives: "Don't do that"; "Don't play with fire"; etc. Negatives are forceful. They are specific, and so they have more impact!

Then, too, even though negative laws set limits beyond which one cannot go, yet they leave one totally free to act within those limits. For instance, a positive law says, "You must drive 60 miles per hour"; that mightily restricts your freedom—you must go 60 m.p.h. no more no less. Whereas a law put negatively preserves freedom; for instance, the law says, "Don't drive over 60 miles per hour"—such a law leaves one free to drive at all speeds under 60 m.p.h. So a law put in the negative preserves freedom. Katherine Lee Bates expresses this aspect of law in her beautiful poem *America*: "...confirm thy soul in self-control / Thy liberty in law." Law is the guardian of liberty.

For Israel, the Ten Commandments were her Bill of Rights. Three defended the rights of God and seven defended the rights of man. The first three protect religion; the last seven protect society.

Commandment Three orders the worship of God. Commandments One and Two remove the obstacles to this worship. One obstacle to worship is error: worshiping false gods. Commandment One removes this error. It proclaims that God is not many, but one God. Monotheism was a startling revelation at this time. That Moses should declare such a truth proves that he must have been speaking with God. For Moses was a child of his world—a world which believed in a host of deities and in gods of all shapes and forms, yet Moses, contrary to all contemporary thinking, proclaimed the astounding message that God is one!

The second obstacle to worship is irreverence—to know there is a one, true God, yet to deny Him worship by bandying His name about as if He didn't exist. Commandment Two removes such irreverence: "Thou shalt not take God's name in vain."

The next seven Commandments preserve society. Commandment Four defends the family, the basis of society. Commandment Five preserves life, Six saves marriage, Seven defends private property, Eight protects the legal system, and Nine and Ten address the heart of man—for good and evil spring from the heart (Mk 7:21-23). Strictly speaking these last two Commandments are not laws but statements of the psychological condition that produces lawlessness. They seek to root out the criminal mentality. Covetousness is that deep self-centeredness that ruthlessly seeks what it wants regardless of the needs and rights of others.

The Covenant was ratified by Israel giving its consent to do all that God commanded. "All that the Lord has said we will heed and do" (24:7).

To seal the Convenant, Moses took the blood of young bulls, part of it he splashed on the altar, then he read the book of the Covenant to the people and they consented. Then he sprinkled the rest of the blood on the people. Finally he and the seventy elders of Israel sat down to a meal (24:5-11).

Blood signified two things: life and kinship. The Hebrews noticed that a dead body does not bleed. They concluded life resided in the blood. Since God gives life, they believed blood was sacred to God and must not be used by man in any way. Thus when animals were sacrificed, a ritual was arranged that the blood be drawn off and offered to God as the first act of the sacrifice. If an animal were killed for food, a priest had to slaughter the animal so that the blood might be returned to God who had given it life. Only such meat was considered fit to eat, was kosher.

Blood also symbolized kinship. Thus persons having the same parents are brothers. Among some Indians, if two persons cut their wrists and mingled the blood, they were supposed to became blood brothers.

Using blood to ratify the Covenant indicated that Israel's life as a nation depended on God and that her consent to His Covenant established a blood-relationship with God, so to speak, making Israel "dearer to God than all other people" (19:5). The ratification of the Covenant was climaxed with a meal; for food nourishes life and to share with others is a sign of brotherliness.

However, keeping the Commandments was not all there was to the Sinaitic Covenant. That was man's side of the Covenant. But there was also God's side. It was this: God promised that if Israel would keep His Commandments, He would be their God and dwell among them. So the remainder of the Book of Exodus (25:1-40:38) is taken up with making a blueprint of God's Dwelling Place among His people and then constructing it according to the plan.

The Covenant made Israel a people, God's people, a nation! At the same time, it obliged God to dwell among His people.

Chapter 8

God's Dwelling and Its Furnishings

As we have already said, there were two sides to God's Covenant with Israel: God's side: I will dwell with you; and man's side: If you keep my Commandments. Chapter 25 to the last chapter of Exodus, Chapter 40, are devoted chiefly to God's Dwelling or Tabernacle. These chapters are divided into three parts. Chapters 25 to 31 contain instructions for building the Dwelling and for its ministers. Chapters 32 to 34 describe Israel's breaking her part of the Covenant and its renewal through the intercession of Moses and Israel's repentance. Chapters 35 to 40 describe the execution of the instructions given in Chapters 25 to 31.

The first directive regarding the Dwelling that God gave Moses was to order him to take up a collection for the materials needed for His Dwelling Place. So eager were the people to have God dwell among them that they gave from their heart enough for the work and more than enough (36:5-7). What they gave in gold, silver, and bronze totaled more than five million dollars. It was as if they were saying that nothing but the best is worthy of God (38:24-31).

Then God showed Moses what His Dwelling was to be; and He commanded Moses to make the Dwelling "exactly according to the pattern that I will now show you" (25:9). Nothing was left to man's wisdom, much less to "chance"; everything was to conform to the model God had shown Moses. This point was so important that no less than four times did God command Moses to make His Dwelling "according to the pattern shown you on the Mount" (Ex 25:9, 40; 26:30; 27:8; Nm 8:4; Acts 7:44; Heb 8:5). Generally when we build something, we begin with the outside then go to the inside. God's ways are not ours. He started the construction of His Dwelling from the inside out.

God started with what was to be the heart of His Dwelling, namely, the **ARK**. The Ark was to be a chest of acacia wood about 4 feet long, 2 1/2 feet wide, and 2 1/2 feet high. It was to be overlaid with pure gold within and without. On the top of the Ark was a lid, a plate of solid gold. Around the bottom of the plate was a crown of gold to prevent it from slipping off the Ark.

This lid was called the propitiatory or "mercy seat" (25:17-22), because the blood of sacrifice sprinkled on it propitiated, appeased the wrath of God (Lv 16:14).

Out of each end of this golden lid a cherub was molded. These two cherubim had wings outstreched, overshadowing the "mercy seat," with their faces looking, down upon it as if in adoration of God.

Yahweh is often referred to as "enthroned upon the cherubim" (1 Sm 4:4; 2 Sm 6:2; Ps 80:2). The Ark was His throne, His footstool, His presence among His people to bless and protect them—His part of the Covenant. The Ark also contained the Ten Commandments—Israel's part of the Covenant. Hence it was called "The Ark of the Covenant." The cherubim were the ministers of God's justice (Gn 3:24). Situated on the "mercy seat," they symbolized that here in the Ark, God's justice and mercy met.

The Ark made of acacia wood and covered with gold typified Jesus with His two natures: the nature of God (the gold) and the nature of man (the acacia wood). The "mercy seat" and the cherubim atop the Ark symbolized the work of Jesus: His redemption, a work of justice and mercy. The two tablets of the Law in the Ark symbolized that Jesus came to fulfill the Law and the prophets (Mt 5:17).

The next furnishing that God directed Moses to build for His Dwelling was a small **TABLE** (25:23-30) of acacia wood, gold plated, with the usual rings and poles for transportation. On it were pitchers for wine, bowls for libation, and incense cups. In addition there were twelve loaves of bread stacked in two piles of six. Every Sabbath the loaves were to be eaten by Aaron and his sons in the Holy Place (Lv 24:5-9) and replaced with twelve others.

A table is connected with food and with eating. The table of the showbread symbolized God and Israel; the eating symbolized Israel's communion with God. This foreshadowed in the New Testament the Lord's table (1 Cor 10:21) and the Lord's supper (1 Cor 11:20).

The third furnishing that God asked Moses to fashion was the **LAMPSTAND** or **MENORAH**. A representation of the Lampstand can be seen on the famous triumphal Arch of Titus in Rome. Also before the Jewish Knesset (Israel's Parliament house in Jerusalem) there is a huge replica of the Lampstand, a gift from the British Parliament in 1966. That Lampstand is made up of panels depicting scenes from Jewish history.

The Lampstand in the Holy Place consisted of one central stem with three lateral branches springing from either side. Each branch was patterned after the branch of the almond tree. The almond tree is the first tree in Palestine to blossom and it has three stages: the bud, the flower, and the fruit. So each branch of the Lampstand was adorned with a bud, with a flower, and finally on top with the fruit, a bowl. The bowl held the oil which fed the lights (25:31-36). The seven-branched Lampstand symbolizes the Church as Light of the Nations through the Holy Spirit in the plenitude of His sevenfold gifts (Rv 1:4). The Holy Spirit is the fruit of Jesus' death (bud), resurrection (flower), and ascension (fruit).

Having shown Moses the contents of the Tabernacle, with the exception of the Altar of Incense (30:1-10), God then proceeded to show him what the Tabernacle which housed these furnishings was to be like. Again God followed His own plan. We would start with the foundation and walls; God started with the roof of the Tabernacle.

The Tabernacle was to be a sort of portable tent having four separate coverings. The first covering was to be made up of fine linen white sheets with cherubim embroidered on them. This covering was protected by three more: one of goatskin, another of rams' skins dyed red, and the outer one of leather.

The Tabernacle was a rectangular wooden-framed building 45 feet long, 15 feet wide, and 15 feet high. The Tabernacle was divided into two parts: the **Holy of Holies** and the **Holy Place**. Only the Ark was in the Holy of Holies, which was a cube 15 feet long, 15 feet wide, and 15 feet high. The Lampstand, the Table, and the Altar of Incense were in the Holy Place, which was 30 feet long, 15 feet wide, and 15 feet high.

The Holy of Holies was separated from the Holy Place by a veil hanging from four pillars. The veil proclaimed that the way to God's presence was not yet manifest. But since it was only a curtain and not a wall of stone or metal, the hint was there that this inaccessibility was only temporary.

The High Priest could pass beyond the veil by the blood of sacrifice on the Day of Atonement, foreshadowing the perfect Sacrifice that would open up the way to God. When Christ died on the cross, this veil was rent from top to bottom showing God was now accessible to man.

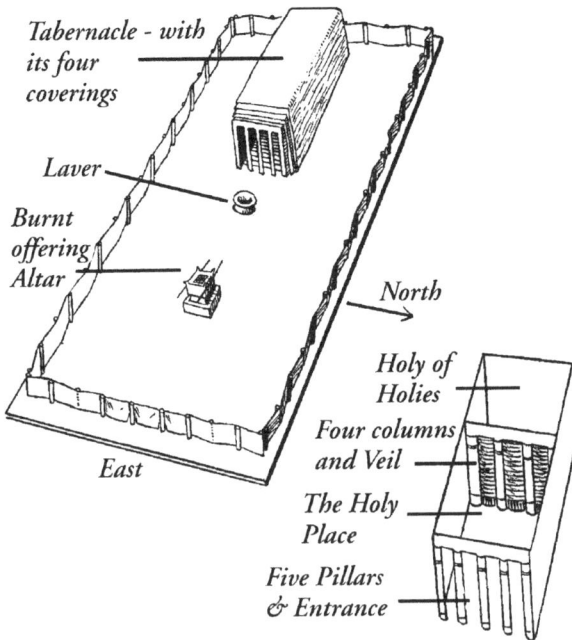

Tabernacle - with its four coverings

Laver

Burnt offering Altar

North →

East

Holy of Holies

Four columns and Veil

The Holy Place

Five Pillars & Entrance

Just before this veil was the ALTAR OF INCENSE (30:1-10). The Altar was about three feet high and square in shape. Incense was offered in the morning and in the evening to the Lord.

Altar of Incense

There was a second veil to the Tabernacle. It was the entrance veil to the Holy Place and was suspended from five pillars. The veil before the Holy of Holies was to bar the way into the Holy of Holies; whereas the entrance veil was to let the priests in to the Holy Place day after day. It was a "door" to the Tabernacle. It was broad, fifteen feet wide. The priestly service of Christ, His sufferings and death, would open the door to the Holy of Holies.

Before the door of the Tabernacle was the Altar of Holocausts (40:6). Between the Altar and the Tabernacle, a bronze Laver filled with water was set up (30:17-21; 40:7).

The **ALTAR OF HOLOCAUSTS** was made of acacia wood, plated with bronze. The Altar was 8 feet long, 8 feet wide, and 5 feet high, covered with a bronze grating. It had rings and poles for transportation. The four corners of the Altar had horns. Horns were the figure of strength and dignity (Ps 132:17)—the image was drawn from bulls that pushed and gored with their horns. In early times horns were converted into trumpets (Jos 6:13) or into flasks for oil (1 Sm 16:1, 13).

The Altar stood in the outer courtyard before the entrance to the Tabernacle, as if to teach us that access to God was to be made by sacrifice. The sinner as it were forfeits his life by sin. To be reconciled to God another life had to be given in the sinner's stead. So the sinner brings an innocent animal and puts his hand on its head before killing it to become identified with it—in this way his sin is transferred to the animal, whereas the animal's innocence is transferrred to the sinner. So the Altar, the symbol of God, became the place where the wages of sin were paid by the shedding of blood. "Without shedding of blood there is no forgiveness" (Heb 9:22).

The **LAVER** (30:17-21) was given last in God's description of the vessels of the Tabernacle because it was to be used only by the priests and so was given after the description of the priests' vestments and consecration (Chapters 28-29).

The Laver was a bronze basin filled with water necessary for ritual purity. The Laver tells of the need of cleansing for communion with God. Even now, we begin Mass with a Penitential Rite.

The Tabernacle, the Altar of Holocaust, and the Laver were all situated in a rectangular Court 150 feet long and 75 feet wide (27:9-18; 38:9-20), entered into by a gate in the east side of the Court. Like medieval towns which were arranged around a cathedral, the tents of the Levites Gershon, Kohath, and Merari, were pitched right next to the western, the southern, and the northern sides of the fence of the Court of the Tabernacle (Nm 3:23, 29, 35).

At some distance from the Levites and encircling them were grouped the twelve tribes: three on each side of the rectangular Court. On the east side, just before the entrance to the Court, were the tents of Moses and Aaron;

behind them the tents of Judah, Issachar, and Zebulun (Nm 2:3-9). On the south side: the tents of Ruben, Simeon, and Gad (Nm 2:10-17) were located. On the west side were the tents of Ephraim, Manasseh, and Benjamin (Nm 2:18-24). On the north side were the tents of Dan, Asher, and Nephtali (Nm 2:25-31). The Tabernacle formed the center of Israel's camp.

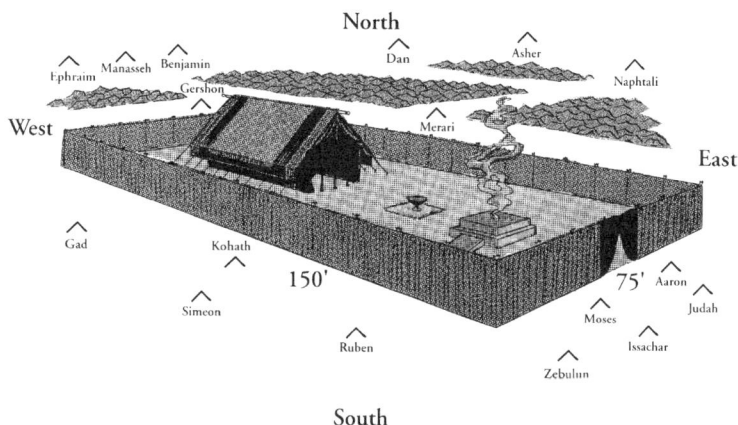

God meant our lives to center around the Blessed Sacrament in the Tabernacle.

Oh, the holiness of God! The entire ritual of Israel's worship emphasized the distance between God and man. One tribe alone was permitted to camp immediately around the Tabernacle, the tribe of Levi.

But another point: God commanded Moses to see to it that the Tabernacle was the center of Israel's encampment. Does this not typify clearly where the Blessed Sacrament should be in our lives and in our churches? Our lives should center around the Blessed Sacrament. And in our churches the Blessed Sacrament should occupy the center place!

Chapter 9

The Priests' Vestments and Consecration

Everything from Chapters 25:10 to 27:19 fore-shadowed God's coming to His people. However, Chapters 27:20 to the end of Chapter 30 reverse the order and point out the provisions which enable man to go to God; namely, the appointment and consecration of priests and the provision for the vessels needed by them to accomplish their work: the Laver and the Altar of Incense.

The high priest, and the other priests, acted as intermediaries between the people and God. This was made evident in the description of the vestments of the high priest. For instance, the names of the twelve tribes were engraved on the two onyx stones on the shoulder straps of the ephod he wore and also on the twelve jewels that were on the breastplate of decision worn over the ephod. His ministry foreshadowed that of Jesus Christ.

The **ephod** was a sleeveless linen garment covering the breast and back, like a scapular. On the shoulder straps were two onyx stones with the names of the twelve tribes of Israel engraved on them, six on each stone.

Over the ephod, was a **breastplate** folded double to form a kind of pouch. In the pouch were the Urim (meaning "light") and Thummim (meaning "perfection")—probably two precious stones, which were used as a lot of some kind to help the priest decide God's will in doubtful matters. His decision lights the way to perfection.

In front of the pouch, four rows of precious stones were mounted—three stones in each row, engraved with the names of the twelve tribes of Israel, signifying they were close to the heart of God.

Underneath the ephod and breastplate the priest wore a blue **robe** of one piece with openings for head and arms. It was to reach just below the knees. Upon the hem of this robe were colored tassels in the form of pomegranetes between each of which was a golden bell. The tinkling of the bells announced to the people that the priest was performing his ministry of intercession. Originally, bells were probably a device to ward off evil spirits.

Beneath the blue robe, the priest wore a long white linen **tunic** brocaded and reaching to the ankles.

Finally, the high priest wore a **miter**, a linen headpiece; to the front of the miter was attached a **plate of pure gold** engraved with the words "Sacred to the Lord." The miter symbolized the high priest's obedience and submission to God's commands.

The sons of Aaron, who were to assist the high priest in the Holy Place, were to wear a long linen tunic, white drawers, a miter wound around the head like a turban but cone shaped, and a sash several yards long wrapped many times around the waist with the ends of the sash draped on the ground, except

when the priest was officiating, then they were thrown over the left shoulder.

Having detailed the vestments that Aaron and his sons were to wear, God described their consecration, that is, the ritual whereby they were to be inducted into the sacred office of priesthood (29:1-46).

Verses 29:1-9 give the preparation for the consecration: the sacrifices to be offered, the ritual bathing of the priests, and the anointing of Aaron.

The ordination rite was completed by a series of animal sacrifices: the sin offering of a young bull (29:10-14); the holocaust of a ram (29:15-18); and the ordination sacrifice of another ram (29:19-28). Before the animals were sacrificed, Aaron and his sons laid their hands on them, thus identifying themselves with the victim. The whole point was that the sinner made satisfaction to God by substitution. The animals sacrificed suffered in place of the sinner.

During the sin offering, the blood of the young bull was used to anoint the altar by touching the horns of the altar with its blood. Next, the first ram was sacrificed: its blood was splashed around the altar; then it was completely burned. Finally, the ordination ram was sacrificed. With its blood Moses touched the tip of Aaron's and his sons' right ear (that they might hear God's commands), their right thumb (that they might do His commands), and their right toe (that they might walk in His way); then its blood was splashed on the sides of the altar and sprinkled on the vestments of Aaron and his sons (29:19-25).

Various portions of this ram were then given to the priests to offer as a "wave offering" before the Lord. In a "wave offering," the priest elevated the parts chosen toward the altar—indicating that they were given to God; and then lowered them to himself—indicating that God returned them to the priests for their sustenance. Then followed a banquet for the priests from the boiled flesh of the ram and the unleavened bread from the basket (29:31-35).

The ordination ceremony was to last seven days. Each day a young bull was offerd as a sin offering.

Chapter 29 Verses 26-30 and 33-46 are later additions. They give the schedule of the daily sacrifices for the entire life of Israel. Two lambs were to be offered each day: one in the morning and the second in the evening. The double animal sacrifices were accompanied each day by libations, cereal, and vegetable offerings.

At the altar God promised to meet the Israelites. His dwelling among them was to be the special sign of His affection for them. As a matter of fact, He delivered His people from slavery in Egypt that He might dwell with them.

In their consecration, Aaron and his sons took no active part. They were passive in the hands of another. They did not minister, but were ministered to. Moses did all at God's commands.

In this way God wished to teach an important lesson regarding the priesthood, namely, the priesthood is an honor no man may assume on his own initiative. A priest is one chosen by God!

Thus when Jesus laid the foundation of His Church, He Himself selected the priests of the New Testament, the twelve apostles. This selective action was so important that Jesus went up to the seclusion of a mountain and prayed the whole night through. Then the next morning, He summoned "those whom HE wanted...HE appointed twelve" (Mk 3:13-14; Lk 6:12-13). In other words, Jesus did the choosing of His apostles! Just because someone may feel that he or she is able to perform the functions of a priest or desires to be a priest gives no one the right to demand ordination to the priesthood. In the final analysis, the priesthood is a vocation: a calling by God—no man may take this honor of himself.

Note: In Chapters 30 and 31 there is a description of the Altar of Incense and the Laver, the making of the oil and the incense. To defray the expenses needed for the upkeep of the Tabernacle, a Census Tax (about 31¢) was levied on every adult over twenty. That was the people's role in their redemption. Finally, God selected the artisans for the building of the Tabernacle, Bezalel, and Oholiab; and lest the work absorb them too completely, God concluded these directives by stating the Sabbath Laws.

Chapter 10

The Covenant, Broken and Renewed

Some have viewed Chapters 32 to 34 as a paren-thesis in the narrative concerning the Tabernacle. They think they interrupt the flow of the Tabernacle theme. This is not so.

When the Israelites arrived at Mt. Sinai (19), Moses went up the mountain to God. God told Moses to tell the people He wished to make a Covenant with them. When Moses did, Israel unanimously accepted God's invitation: "Everything the Lord has said we will do" (19:8). When Moses brought back Israel's response to the Lord, God had them prepare for three days. On the third day, God manifested Himself with peals of thunder and lightning and trumpet blasts. A heavy cloud came over the mountain and smoke rose from it as from a furnace. Then God delivered the Ten Commandments of the Covenant (20:1). When Moses related all that God had asked of His people, they answered with one voice, "We will do everything the Lord has told us" (24:3). Then Moses solemnly ratified the Covenant by blood (24:4-8). All this was done orally within a matter of a few days.

After the ratification of the Covenant, God said to Moses: "Come up to me on the mountain…and I will give you the stone tablets on which I have written the commandments….After Moses had gone up, a cloud covered the mountain. The glory of the Lord settled upon Mount Sinai. The cloud covered it for six days and on the seventh day…Moses passed into the midst of the cloud as he went up the mountain; and there he stayed for forty days and forty nights" (24:12-18).

In those forty days God instructed Moses about

building the marvelous and mysterious Tabernacle as His Dwelling Place. Then He showed him the pattern of the things that were to be constructed. He did all this in Chapters 25 to 31.

While Moses was receiving these divine revelations up on the mountain, Chapters 32 to 34 tell us what the people were doing down at the foot of the mountain. They were breaking the Covenant.

It happened this way. When Moses did not come down from the mountain immediately, the people went to Aaron and said, "Come make us a god who will be our leader; as for the man Moses who brought us out of the land of Egypt, we do not know what has happened to him" (32:1).

The Israelites had missed the whole point of God's interventions in Egypt on their behalf. They attributed all to Moses. And they even referred to Moses contemptuously as "the man Moses." When man turns away from the one true God, he makes his own gods. So the people told Aaron "make us a god." Aaron made a golden calf. The calf, or ox, was the principal Egyptian god—Apis; the god they were familiar with while in slavery in Egypt. "They made a calf in Horeb and adored a molten image;…They forgot the God who had saved them, who had done great deeds in Egypt" (Ps 106:19, 21).

God got very angry with them. After all He had done for them, they turned their backs on Him. So God told Moses, "Go down at once to **your** people, whom **you** brought out of the land of Egypt…." God was being very sarcastic: "**your** people…**you** brought out"! God went on to say, "I see how stiff-necked this people is"; stiff-necked, that is, how self-willed they are, unwilling to submit to obedience to my will. "Let me destroy them," God said in anger to Moses. "Then I will make of you a great nation" (32:10).

EXODUS: ROAD TO FREEDOM

How angry God was! Yet Moses stood up to God. Even though Moses had received only ingratitude from the people, he loved them and so he interceded for them.

First, he set the record straight with God. He wouldn't, so to speak, let God pass the buck to him. This people was not his people but God's people—"your own people whom you brought out of the land of Egypt with such great power and with so strong a hand" (32:11). Moses reminded God that it was He who had redeemed Israel through no merit of their own, but out of His sheer wonderful grace and graciousness.

Next Moses argued with God not to destroy His people because this would create a false image of Himself with the Egyptians. "The Lord is good and kind—slow to anger, forgiving," Moses reasoned. But if He destroyed His people, the Egyptians would put Him in a class with their own false gods who were cruel, vengeful and punitive (Nm 14:13-18). This could not be.

Finally, Moses appealed to God's fidelity, "Remember your servants Abraham, Isaac, and Israel, and how you swore to them by your own self, saying, 'I will make your descendants as numerous as the stars in the sky, and all this land that I promised, I will give your descendants...' " (32:13). Moses argued that God could not go back on His promises. Israel might renege on the Covenant, but not God, for He is good and faithful.

Moses won out. God heard his prayers. "The Lord relented in the punishment he had threatened to inflict on his people" (32:14)—so once again He calls them "**His** people."

What lessons we have here.

First, how wonderful it was for Israel to have such an intercessor with God as Moses. They sensed the great gap between God and themselves. "You speak to us and we will listen," they begged Moses; "but let not God speak to us, or we shall die" (20:19). Moses did and his pleading for Israel saved the nation.

How foolish it is that some attack praying to Mary and the saints! God has always used intercessors between Himself and mankind. He gave Israel Moses and the prophets and He has given us the Saints, Mary and Jesus (1 Tm 2:5). It is important that we pray to them. Jesus promised that what we ask in His name will be given us (Jn 14:13). So the Church in Her liturgy concludes Her prayers "through Christ our Lord." St. Bernard wrote that "never was it known that anyone who sought the intercession of Mary was left unaided."

Second, Moses reminded God of His promises to Abraham, Isaac, and Israel. We ought to remind ourselves of God's promises to us regarding prayer. Jesus said, "Ask and you shall receive; seek and you shall find; knock and it shall be opened to you" (Lk 11:9). This one promise of Jesus ought to fill us with confidence in prayer, and confidence is one of the keys to effective prayer.

After Moses had successfully mediated for the people, he started down the mountain with the two tablets of the Commandments inscribed by God's own finger (31:18). When he came to the camp and saw the golden calf and the obscene dancing around it, Moses' wrath flared up and he flung the tablets of stone to the ground, smashing them. Then he ground the golden calf to powder, which he scattered on the stream that flowed down the side of Mt. Sinai and made the Israelites drink the polluted water. Next he upbraided Aaron for giving in to the people. Finally, he called upon the Levites to slay the guilty—that day about three thousand of the people were slain.

How often, like Aaron, people give in to peer pressure, doing things that they know are wrong, abandoning God's law for idols—money, pleasure, going along to get along, making compromises because people demand them. What a contrast between Aaron and Moses! Aaron complied with the sinful demands of people; but Moses, single-handed, stood up against the entire community in defense of the Law of God and prevailed. "Moses was faithful in all God's household" (Heb 3:5).

On the next day Moses said to the people, "You have committed a grave sin. I will go up to the Lord, then; perhaps I may be able to make atonement for your sin" (32:30). Moses used the word "perhaps" because as yet the people did not show any repentance or contrition for their grave sins.

Still Moses returned to the Lord. Moses was preeminently a man of prayer. In every crisis we find him turning back to God. He was intensely devoted not only to God but to God's people. Even though the people did not appreciate him, even though they repeatedly murmured and rebelled against him, their utter unworthiness could not quench his love for and devotion to them. No sin on their part could alienate his affections for them. So Moses tells God, "If you will not forgive them, then strike me out of the book you have written" (32:32). Great as Moses' mediation and love for God's people were, they are nothing compared to the love of Mary and the Saints and especially of Jesus for us.

Moses' mediation won from God immediate safety for the people and the promise of an angelic guide and protection during their journey to the Promised Land. Despite this promise, God still chastised them when they sinned. For God afflicts neither willingly nor arbitrarily, but only to purify and sanctify—"whom the Lord loves, he disciplines" (Heb 12:6).

Had there been no Moses to plead the cause of Israel, it would have most certainly perished, just as the world would most certainly have perished had we not had

Jesus to live and make intercession for us (Heb 7:25).

Because Israel remained a stiff-necked people, and did not repent for their sins, God threatened not to accompany them nor dwell in their midst. Moses took the tabernacle—not the one with the Ark and the three furnishings in the Holy Place for these had not yet been built—and erected it outside the camp. It was a Tent of Meeting, the place where God and people could meet. Removing the Tent outside the camp moved Israel to sorrow. To show their repentance, they laid aside their ornaments (33:6).

Now Israel's repentance gave Moses a leg to stand on with God. So once again he pleaded with God to dwell with His people and accompany them to the Promised Land. This request the Lord promised to carry out because Moses was His friend (33:17).

Moses had asked two things of God: to avert His wrath from Israel and to continue to dwell among them. God granted both requests. Emboldened, Moses made a third request: "Let me see your glory." What is the Lord's glory? It is His mercy! The Lord cried out: "The Lord, the Lord, a merciful and gracious God, slow to anger and rich in kindness and fidelity, continuing his kindness for a thousand generations, and forgiving wickedness and crime and sin…" (34:6-7).

The first part of Exodus, from Egypt to Sinai, was done out of God's sheer grace. Israel merited nothing. They were no better than the Egyptians. Yet God freed them from slavery, fed them in the desert, gave them victory over their enemies, the Egyptian army and the Amalekites—all through no merit of their own (cp. Ps 105).

And how did they respond to His graces? "They remembered not your abundant kindness, but rebelled against the Most High…they tempted God in the wilderness…they envied Moses…they made a golden calf in

Horeb...they murmured in their tents..." (Ps 106). But Moses pleaded for them and God revealed to him the richest of His attributes: His mercy—man's extremity, God's opportunity. After Sinai Israel never sings of God's grace, but only of His mercy—that quality in God's nature that meets the deep and dire needs of those who have sinned against His grace. The background of grace is our poverty, our emptiness, our worthlessness. The foil for His mercy is our sinfulness, our wickedness, our vileness!

On June 13, 1929, at midnight, in the chapel of the Dorothean convent of Tuy, Sister Lucia had a sublime vision of the Holy Trinity and the Immaculate Heart of Mary, in which the consecration of Russia was requested.

In this vision, Sister Lucia saw the Father as a man from the waist up; at His chest, she saw the Holy Spirit as a dove; and beneath the Holy Spirit was Christ crucified. Under His right arm was Our Lady of Fatima. Under His left arm, large letters appeared, made of crystal-clear water running onto the altar, forming these words: "Grace and Mercy." The significance of the words "Grace" and "Mercy" was this. God first gives His people grace; but when they reject it, He has nothing left to give them but His mercy.

In the first part of Exodus, for instance, all God gave Israel sprang from His grace and graciousness. Israel revolted against God. Moses' prayer averted Israel's destruction; all God could give them now was His mercy.

Like Israel, Christians have been rejecting God's graces. Our sins today are worse than those of Sodom and Gomorrha. All that remains for us is to turn to God's mercy. That was the message God entrusted to Blessed Mary Faustina.

The Latin word for mercy is <u>misericordia</u> which comes from two Latin words: <u>miseri</u> meaning "misery" and <u>cordia</u> meaning "heart." Mercy means "having a heart for the miseries of others and doing something about it." The greatest misery is sin, the rejection of God's graces; the greatest mercy is God stooping down by His Incarnation and Redemption to lift up the sinner and restore him to grace.

Because God is merciful, Moses prayed for Israel, "Pardon our sins and take us for your own." God answered his prayer and took Israel for His inheritance (Ps 94:14). He renewed the Covenant, and He promised even greater wonders than those in Egypt, like clearing out the Promised Land of its inhabitants. But He warned Israel not to intermarry with the inhabitants nor to make a covenant with them, but to destroy their altars and their idols (34:10-17).

Because nature abhors a vacuum, it is never enough to get rid of a false religion; a true religion must take its place, so God commanded Israel to have its own religious celebrations. They must have the feast of Unleavend Bread (Passover); they must consecrate their first-born, both of men and of beasts, to the Lord; they must observe the Sabbath; celebrate the feast of Weeks (Pentecost, Lv 23:15-21); and a harvest feast at the close of the year (the feast of Tabernacles, Dt 16:16).

The last six Chapters of Exodus 35-40 deal with the execution of all the things God had shown Moses on the Mount in Chapters 25-31—the actual construction of His Tabernacle.

First, the Israelites were commanded to observe the Sabbath. Before we work for God, we must rest in God. Before we can do, we must receive power from on high (35:1-3).

Next, material was gathered for the construction of the Tabernacle. All the material was to be given freely, as one's heart prompted (35:4-29).

Then the Tabernacle was constructed according to the pattern God showed Moses on the Mount. The vestments for Aaron and his sons were all made "as the Lord had commanded Moses." That expression "as the Lord had commanded" occurs eight times in Chapter 39 and seven times in Chapter 40. Like Moses and the Israelites in those instances, we too should be obedient to all that God commands us.

When all was done, "the cloud covered the meeting tent and the glory of the Lord filled the Dwelling" (40:34).

God enters every open door: when the Tabernacle was finished, the cloud, the symbol of God's presence, descended upon it. Also, when our hearts are opened, God comes in.

APPENDIX

In the Old Testament, once a year on the Feast of Yom Kippur, the High Priest slew a young bull for its blood. Then he took the blood and sprinkled it on the mercy seat in the Holy of Holies. Then he returned to the Altar of Holocaust in the courtyard and sprinkled the blood on the Altar as a sign of reconciliation with God.

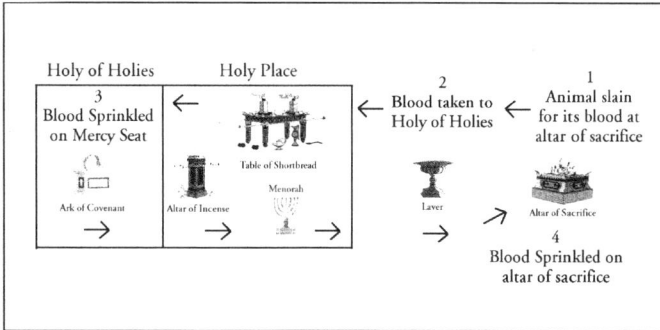

This annual action typified the sacrifice of the High Priest in the New Testament, Jesus Christ. On the cross on Calvary, He shed His blood. Then after His resurrection, He ascended to Heaven to enter the Holy of Holies and at the right hand of the Father offer His sacrifice for our salvation. Then He returns from the Holy of Holies to the Altars of earth to bring reconciliation to man and God by the sacrifice of the Mass.

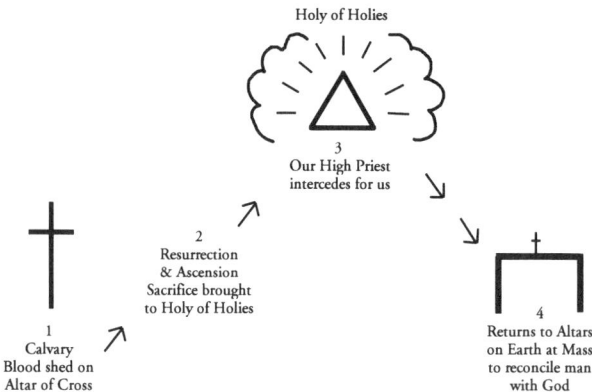

Hebrews 9:3-12